W9-BOP-752

PRESENTED TO

BY

DATE

J. Countryman

Nashville, Tennessee

The
Reel Line

An
Angler's
Guide
to the
Ultimate
Catch

Jimmy Houston

The
Reel Line

Published by J. Countryman®, a division of Thomas Nelson, Inc., Nashville, Tennessee 37214

Designed by Koechel-Peterson and Associates, Minneapolis, Minnesota

Project editor: Jenny Baumgartner

ISBN 0-8499-5758-3

Printed and bound in Belgium

www.jcountryman.com

Acknowledgements

Special thanks to Dr. Andy Bowman who prepared the "Catch of the Day" segments of this book.

Andy Bowman is the pastor of the First Baptist Church of Keys, Oklahoma. He has served full-time in the ministry for twenty-seven years with pastorates in Oklahoma, Alabama, and Florida. He received his doctorate in Christian Counseling from Luther Rice Bible College and Seminary in Georgia. He and his wife, Renie, have been married for twenty-eight years, and they have two children and two grandchildren. Andy praises God daily for the wonderments and blessings of the Father.

Table of Contents

Foreword

Al Lindner

Two of the things Jimmy Houston and I unquestionably have in common are a love for the Lord and an obvious love for the sport of fishing. Both of us were blessed by God with the opportunity to make a living in a sport we enjoy as well as reaching people for Jesus Christ while doing it.

In the New Testament, both Jesus and Paul took everyday experiences from peoples' lives and used them as parables to illustrate and explain the workings of the kingdom of God. Jesus frequently taught spiritual lessons by referring to common events found at work and home and in social interactions. Some of His parables are crystal clear in meaning, while others require spiritual discernment. Similarly, the apostle Paul

used numerous examples from the sports world to illustrate how believers should live their spiritual lives.

Sportfishing—much like football, golf, car racing, and other activities— is teeming with life lessons. These lessons, when viewed through God's prism, can become very effective modern-day parables. When my brother Ron speaks to other fishermen about how he came to faith in Jesus Christ, he often talks about "being scooped up by the gentle net of God's grace." He also says that "God does not practice catch and release. Instead, He puts us in His live well of eternal life—forever." It's these real-life illustrations that plainly and clearly show how God works today!

As you read this book, you'll be inspired and encouraged by the way that Jimmy uses many of the fishing experiences from his long and successful career to illustrate and teach spiritual principles from the Word of God. You'll also see how God is at work in even the most routine acts of our lives. And, you'll catch some great fishing secrets as well.

Good fishing!

Al Lindner
In-Fisherman, Inc.

Chapter 1

The Details

Several years ago, my wife, Chris, participated in a Project Sports tournament on Lake Ouachita in Arkansas. On the first day, she was paired with a very nice doctor from Hot Springs, Arkansas. He didn't have much tournament experience, though, and he was having a tough day catching fish.

At about noon, the doctor excitedly told Chris that he had seen a big bass swirl to the right of the boat, toward the middle of the pocket they were fishing. Chris had seen a turtle's head in that area before it ducked out of sight and knew it was not a bass. She told the doctor it was just a turtle and continued to cast the shoreline and ignore the swirl. The doctor decided to throw his lure to the spot, and . . . Bang! A bass over six pounds inhaled his bait. It turned out to be the biggest fish of the day.

Obviously, many lessons can be learned from this experience. The one that first comes to mind is to pay attention to everything that happens during the fishing day. Observe everything that is going on, no matter how small. Look for clues about where to throw or how to catch a fish. Also keep an eye out for any movement in the water—for a bush shaking or a piece of grass or a reed that moves.

Also look for baitfish—if a shad or minnow jumps out of the water, then a larger fish is probably after it. Also watch closely for any birds that are feeding because they can give you an indication of baitfish in the area. Paying attention to these little things might give you a big catch.

Jesus told us that if we are diligent in small matters, then He will put us in charge of big matters. Nowhere is this more important than in our relationships with others, especially with family and close friends. We need to pay special attention to little things that are important to others, such as noticing that your wife just had her hair done or your son has cleaned his room. A little thing like noticing now nice your neighbor's flower garden looks can mean so much.

A good tip to remember is to ask about people's kids. Be genuine in your handling of these small details. Pay attention to the fine points out of love. After all, because He loves us, God pays attention to every detail in our lives, no matter how small, no matter how big.

Too often, the big picture clouds our outlook on a given situation. When fishing, we sometimes don't even realize all of the small details that led to a catch. Closely watch all of the little things that are going on around you on the lake. To have a better personal relationship with those around you, simply do the same thing.

Catch of the Day

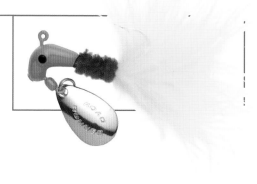

Sometimes we think that only major events really have meaning, but Elijah didn't hear from God in the wind or the fire, or even the earthquake that God inhabited. Instead, he heard the "still small voice" of God.

If we spend all of our time attending to only the more pressing things in our lives, we can miss out on a great deal of

. . . and after

the fire

a still

small voice.

I KINGS 19:12

life. What seems so vital isn't always so very important. Jesus even taught that a small cup of water given in His name is special.

Don't overlook God's great blessings that may come in silence while you are occupying yourself with things that are loud and spectacular.

Chapter 2

Ripraps

Ripraps are one of my favorite places to fish. These manmade rock structures are perfect hiding places for crawdads and small baitfish, such as bluegill, and shad love to feed on the algae that grows on them. These two things combined make rip rap a natural attractant for bass.

It is a good idea to stop and fish any riprap you may pass, no matter how small or how large. Fish constantly move up and down on riprap. It's sometimes difficult to pattern the bass to be there at a certain time, but you can be sure that sometime during the day, bass will feed on the rocks. You just need to be there at the same time the bass are.

I've caught literally hundreds of bass on riprap, but one day on Lake Tenkiller really stands out as a great learning experience. Tenkiller has only one bridge that crosses the Illinois River in the upper end of the lake, and one side of the bridge has rip rap. We were fishing in a small local tournament that took off out of the Caney Creek dock less than a mile from that bridge. I raced to that riprap and caught a nice ten bass limit in less than fifteen minutes on a small crawdad-colored Bomber crankbait. I had a limit while some of the guys were still running to their spots.

I culled a few fish throughout the day and easily won the tournament. Had I not started my day on that riprap, though, I most certainly would have lost. The key was being at the right place at the right time.

Our lives depend on being at the right place at the right time. I believe God orchestrates these situations in order to do great things in our lives. I call them "divine appointments," and as a Christian, I believe divine appointments happen all the time. Sometimes God arranges them to help us in our relationships with others. Some are planned in order to help further our careers or to provide business opportunities that allow God to pour down His rich blessings on us.

Other divine appointments have a higher calling. They are those circumstances and meetings that God arranges in order to use us for His purposes. He may use us to share our faith and the Gospel of Jesus in order to save a lost soul. God may also use us to help bear another Christian's problems, or He may use other Christians to share in our struggles.

Jesus promised to be with us always, even until the end of the age. He'll use His divine appointments to meet our needs and the needs of all of

His children. Being on that riprap at just the right time produced a winning catch for me, and I believe God places us at the right place at the right time—with the right people—to produce winning Christians.

Catch of the Day

*T*he children's song says, "Be careful little feet where you go . . ." This is an important lesson for adults, too. We should make certain that our travels are taking us where God is leading us. God promises that He will guide us to places that will bless us and honor Him if we are obedient.

Our compass may not always point "true north" because we have our own plans and agendas. However, when we are obedient, we are smack dab in the middle of where He wants us to be. There, He sets up divine appointments.

> *In all thy ways acknowledge Him and He shall direct thy paths.*
>
> PROVERBS 3:6

When He's guiding, leading, and providing, we feel wonderful. When we're in charge of our lives, we may feel that we're missing out on life's very best. You may want to ask yourself, *Am I keeping my divine appointments?*

Chapter 3

Logs and Lay Downs

A bank lined with logs and lay downs will stop almost any bass fisherman. In fact, about every boat that comes by will spend some time chunking at this cover. Fallen trees provide great ambush places for bass and offer several potential strike zones. The older the log the better. Old trees and logs that have lost all their bark are really killers.

Bass seem to like hardwoods such as oaks and sycamores better than pine trees. In fact, a pine tree is almost never any good until it is slick from losing all its bark. This sometimes takes years for a pine tree, but an oak or sycamore can produce bass the same day it falls or is placed in the lake.

While these areas with a lot of logs and lay downs are good fishing locations, the very best place to fish is an isolated log. If you take the time to search out that individual log, you will almost always be rewarded with a bass.

Lonely logs are prime fishing spots, but a lonely person faces an almost unbearable daily struggle. God never intended for us to be alone. Shortly after creating man, God created woman and commanded them to start a family. He didn't encourage them to do so or even ask them— He *commanded* them.

One of the biggest tragedies today is the breakup of the family. It's even more tragic to see the divorce rate among Christians mirror the divorce

rate of the rest of society. God hates divorce, yet Christian families split apart every day. Chris and I got married when we were teenagers. Now after thirty-seven years, our marriage is stronger than ever. I've certainly been a less-than-perfect husband, but through it all, God's love has kept this family together.

A total commitment to God allows nothing less than a total commitment to your wife or husband and to your kids. The way to have a closer and stronger relationship with your spouse is to have a closer and stronger relationship with God. That means striving to please God in everything we do, say, and think. If we are pleasing God, then we will be doing and saying the kind of things that will please our wife or husband.

Faithfulness in a marriage is a given. God is very explicit; He says, "Thou shalt not commit adultery." But that's not the whole ballgame. It's tantamount to be loving and supportive in all circumstances, even when our mate fails or disappoints us. After all, that's how Jesus is with each of us.

It's equally important to express our love and commitment with words and actions. The easiest person to take for granted is a husband or wife. Let your spouse know every single day just how important and special he or she really is.

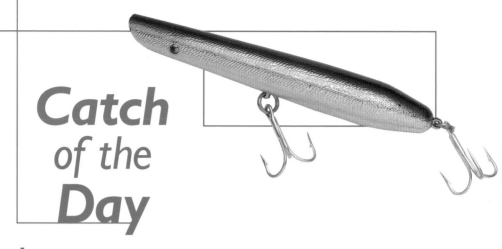

Catch
of the
Day

Love takes on a variety of faces. To most folks, love can be spelled T-I-M-E. If we don't take the time—or make the time, rather—for our family, we're actually showing them we don't truly love them. We seem to be able to have time for things we truly want to do, like fishing, but your family must be at the top of your priorities. How do they know you really care if you aren't present?

Some families suffer with identity crises because Dad is never around. He's just too busy with other things to be really involved with his family. But isn't that why we marry and have children—because we desire true relationships? TIME—make time for those who are important, before it all runs out.

> Husbands,
>
> love your
>
> wives . . .
>
> EPHESIANS 5:25

Chapter 4

Button Willows

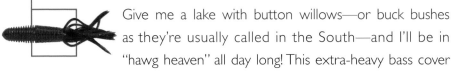

Give me a lake with button willows—or buck bushes as they're usually called in the South—and I'll be in "hawg heaven" all day long! This extra-heavy bass cover is usually at its best when the lake is a little high because plenty of water is under the willows. Two years in a row in B.A.S.S. tournaments on Lake Sam Rayburn in Texas, I finished in the top five—one in second place and one in third place—by fishing nothing but buck brushes. My good friend Denny Brauer won both tournaments, and he also fished buck bushes in pretty much the same area I did.

The trick to catching bass from these bushes is to get your bait into the "heart" of the bush—not around the edges or close to the buck bush, but right down in the very middle of it. I like to use a ¼ or ½ ounce Terminator jig with a frog chunk trailer or a Riverside tube rigged either in a jig head or Texas rigged. My jig choice is usually a black/blue/purple with a frog chunk. My tube preference is pumpkin-pepper, although I use a variety of green, blue, and red combinations.

In this cover, most bass can get off the hook because it's too small, so I prefer to use a good size hook, such as a 4/0 or 5/0 Owner hook. Chris and I fish a lot of 17 pound test line in these bushes, but you'll probably be better off with 20 to 25 pound test. We use green Trilene XT.

We cast a lot to this type cover, but mostly we use a flippin' or pitching technique to get our baits into the heart of the bushes. One of the keys to being really successful on this structure is to fish quickly. Put that bait into the heart of the cover and let it sink. If a bass doesn't have it by the time it hits the bottom, it's generally best to pick it up and put it in another bush. Most bites will be on the initial drop.

Just as the bass lives in the heart of a buck bush, Jesus lives in the heart of every Christian. When that fish moves out of that bush, he becomes more susceptible to danger, which is also true for Christians who do not stay within Christ's protection.

It's easy to push Jesus aside, and we can do this in so many ways. We can do it by choosing to run around with people who are living for the world. It's easy to conform to their standards rather than follow the standards of Jesus. We also do it by letting anger, jealousy, or so many other evils control our values or ethics in a business deal or personal

relationship. We can also do it by failing to read God's Word and not going to God's church.

These and so many other things remove Jesus from our focus. When this happens, the devil is eager to jump in and take control. Amazingly, our Jesus is always ready to help us refocus our heart with His love. We need only to repent.

Catch *of the* **Day**

We all have a tough time squeezing everything we want to do into a normal day. Between work and family and deadlines and Little League, we run out of daylight before we run out of projects.

Perhaps that's why the Word of God calls on us to pray continually. We aren't asked to fall down and pray and ignore the other issues of life. He isn't commanding believers to neglect anything.

Instead, He's commanding us to be in an attitude and spirit of prayer twenty-four hours a day and seven days a week. This pattern helps you to open prayer early and keep it open until late.

> *Pray without*
>
> *ceasing . . .*
>
> I THESSALONIANS 5:17

We should start each day with "Good morning, Lord," and remember that all we do or say that day is a part of that prayer. When we pray continually, there is plenty of time for all we do.

Chapter 5

Rocks

Largemouth, spotted, and smallmouth bass love rocks. In fact, just about every great smallmouth- or spotted-bass lake has an abundance of good rocky cover. There are, of course, a lot of ways to fish rocks successfully, but the key is figuring out how the bass are positioned on or around the rocks. The time of the year, the type of rock structure, and whether or not there is a current are your keys to knowing how bass position themselves on rocks. It is easy to read the current. Bass must face into the current and will seek out eddy areas behind the rocks to hide, relax, and wait for food to drift by. All you need to do is cast upstream of the rocks and let the current carry your lure to the fish just like with natural bait.

Early in the year, around spawning season, a bass will build its bed and spawn near solitary rocks or boulders. Find the single rocks, and you'll soon find spawning beds. Even if you can't see the bed but you can see the rock, there's probably a fish there.

Concentrate on rock bluffs and ledges in the summer and fall. Sheer bluffs will always have ledges that hold bass. The water may be forty to fifty feet deep or deeper, but the small ledges that are ten to twenty feet deep can be loaded with bass.

Also look for the opposite of ledges—holes back in the bluffs and steep banks. These are some of my favorite places to find bass in the fall and early winter months. Jigs and crawdad-colored crankbaits are

dynamite here. If you're into live bait, live crawdads will mean instant fish on these bluffs.

Rocks are an important part of life to bass . . . and to humans. Rocky times will come into everyone's life. They can come in the form of simple inconveniences, family feuds and spats with friends, financial problems, or illness and death. Over the years, I've found that many rough spots weren't really that tough at all. I look back on some of my most pressing problems and find that they were really benefits disguised as problems.

Jesus told us not to worry about yesterday, today, or tomorrow. God already knows what we need and is already taking care of it. My problem, though, is that I often want what I don't need. I easily forget that God will supply my needs, not necessarily my wants.

But what about the giant rocks of sickness and death? I can't imagine anyone even attempting to face these without a close personal relationship with Jesus Christ. God is the Great Physician. He will heal His own—some He will heal here on earth, but everyone will be healed in

heaven. He has promised that there will be no tears, no blindness, and no sickness in heaven.

Death has been overcome by Jesus right here on earth. When Jesus rose from that grave, He ascended to heaven and promised every Christian that where He is going, we will be going also—and we'll go there alive!

Catch of the Day

Trust is the greatest divider of people when it comes to troubles. In what or whom do we put our trust when things get rough?

The world systems of self-sufficiency, indifference, humanism, and entitlements don't offer a lot of solace or peace when rocks seem to cave in around us. It's tough to trust in people at difficult times.

> I will never leave you nor forsake you.
>
> HEBREWS 13:5

Isn't it wonderful that as believers, we can trust God and His promises? He said that no matter what we go through, He'll go, too. He has promised comfort, understanding, and His presence to those who know Him.

As the songwriter said some years ago, "Many things about tomorrow I don't seem to understand, but I know Who holds tomorrow . . . " If He holds your life, your world, and your tomorrows, then you can trust Him to handle the rocks.

Chapter 6

Points

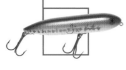

I've often said even if you didn't know anything about bass fishing at all, you could simply start fishing every point you saw, and you'd have a good chance of finding bass. No matter how much you know, when all else fails, fishing a point will usually provide some action.

A point is an outcropping of anything (not necessarily land) that juts out into the water. The time of the year, weather, and type of point I'm fishing will dictate my technique and lure choices. One of the easiest ways to locate fish on any larger point is to troll over it. This lets you cover a lot of water quickly, and you can isolate the places and depths that hold fish. Pay close attention to your locator and always have marker buoys handy. When you catch a fish, throw that marker overboard and study your locator. A slow pass or two by that marker while studying your fish locator should tell you if and why the bass are there. They could be attracted to a rock, a brushpile, an old tree, or a drop-off. Isolating that spot sometimes produces a huge catch. Not all points are big, however. Some are tiny—so tiny that you can fish the entire point with just one cast. Keep a sharp eye out for these small points.

I like to troll the shallow points with a rattling Hot Spot and the deeper ones with a Bomber or Rebel crankbait. When trolling, make sure your bait is running straight. Another of my favorite lures for deep points is a Heddon Zara Spook. This topwater is especially dynamite after the

spawn but really works all the way to late fall. The clearer the water, the deeper a bass will come up to eat that spook.

I use buoys to mark a point in the lake so that I can remember it. I also believe in marking all over any Bible I read, underlining passages that are meaningful to me and constantly making notes to myself about what God is telling me. Most of these notes and underlines I never see again because I use several Bibles. I usually give away my daily Bible—the one I read through completely in a year—after I've marked in it. These marks show important messages from God to me as I read His Word. The Bible is not just a compilation of words like a novel; it is the Living Word of God.

Does God throw out marker buoys? I believe He does. You can test this for yourself. The next time you have a problem or a need, simply pick

up a Bible, open it up, and start reading. I'm willing to bet that God will mark the answers and lead you to them. Sometimes it takes only one small verse out of the whole Bible. Too often we struggle for answers to problems and needs when God's Word has the solution right at our fingertips.

Catch *of the* Day

*A*nswers for today's problems can't be found in the newspapers or magazines that we frequently read. We don't have the wisdom to shed much truth into our troubled waters.

The Psalmist realized that whenever God spoke, it would be worthwhile to listen. Whatever God said would be for His benefit.

The Bible isn't a book of rules of dos and don'ts; it's a book to guide and share life. It provides a true assessment on how we should handle life's situations.

> You are near, O Lord, and all Your commandments are truth.
>
> PSALM 119:151

The truths it holds don't change with public opinion or convenience. In fact, when we are all gone and the things we hold dear have faded away, God's Word will still be marking the way on the waters of life.

Chapter 7

Deep Water Structure

Deep water is perhaps one of the most misunderstood and least fished areas of the lake. Even though we all know there are a lot of fish in the deep, we don't spend too much time trying to figure out how to fish those areas. Here are three easy steps to help.

First, you have to understand what you are seeing. Twenty-feet deep is the same as the distance from the front of my Ranger boat to the back. That's not much distance after all.

Second, mark out the deep-water structure you want to fish with marker buoys. This immediately lets you analyze how this structure looks from a different perspective. A ledge or creek channel is much easier to understand and fish when you see it laid out with buoys on the water's surface.

Third, use a good fish locator and learn how to interpret what you are seeing on the screen. I use a Humminbird liquid crystal graph on both the console and the bow. I also have a Zercom flasher on the console. My front transducer is mounted on the front of my Motor Guide trolling motor, and my console transducers are in the back. This gives me not one, but three looks at what's under my boat.

After these three steps, you're on your way to a good catch in deep water, but you need one more element to help you: you need to add

the "Big P"—patience. You've got to be really patient and learn how to fish deep water successfully. The best way to learn deep-water structure is to leave all your lures, rods, and reels at home; then go to the lake and start looking and learning.

According to God's Word, patience is a virtue. I've found that as I've grown older, patience is a little easier to come by. When I was younger, I did not have patience, and I really didn't want it. If patience is godly, how do we go about obtaining it?

Most importantly, we've got to realize patience usually will not come about automatically. We have a tendency to get angry too quickly with our husband, wife, friends, or enemies. We sometimes do not have the time to allow our kids to work through a problem; instead, we go ahead and solve it for them, thus depriving them of a needed growing experience.

How often do we want God to answer a prayer right now even though the Bible tells us to wait patiently on the Lord? We know God will answer on His time schedule and not ours. After all, His time will always be best. Since it is usually difficult for us to be patient, He will work patience in us. But we need to stop fighting Him about it. The whole process becomes easier when we finally and totally realize that our Heavenly Father knows best.

Catch
of the
Day

When we wait, it usually feels like a waste of time. We'd rather be doing something that seems more vital to our lives. However, from a biblical perspective, "wait" signifies a desire to serve Him, much like a waiter in a restaurant waits on or serves his customers.

God seeks our very best in every situation, every time. He wants to accomplish good for us and bring glory to Himself, and He will do it if we wait on Him.

> *They that wait on the Lord will find new strength...*
>
> ISAIAH 40:31 (NLB)

Chapter 8

Stumps

At a B.A.S.S. tournament on Lake Gaston in southern Virginia several years ago, I learned a valuable lesson in fishing stumps that has paid off quite a few times since. The creek where I found the fish had quite a few boat docks and a small number of stumps. I caught a bass every now and then off a dock but not many.

Bass seem to like anything different. When I found one of those isolated stumps, just about every one held a fish. But the stumps were hard to see in the dingy water, and I had to "bump the stump" with my spinnerbait in order to trigger the strike. It was almost impossible to see my bait well enough to bump the stump correctly and not hang up. I found a solution to the problem: a white blade on the spinnerbait. This let me see the blade just enough to fish the stump and get a nice check for a top ten finish.

The best stumps are the ones that are the most difficult to see; they are missed by most other fishermen. I particularly like stumps that are on the edge of a creek channel or drop-off. The stump closest to the edge of the drop usually will hold the biggest bass. If you catch a bass off a stump, remember that stump. Some are special holding spots and will have a fish on it pretty much every time you fish it. Even when the water is higher and you can't see the stump, there will still be a fish there if you can remember where it is and how it needs to be fished. When the water drops and that "special stump" is high and dry, go take a closer look and

see what's so special about it. This will give you a clue as to how to fish it when the water rises again.

Taking a closer look at our relationships with our family and friends will give us a better idea about how to make those relationships happier and more meaningful. Most of the time, I've found that when I'm having a problem getting along with someone as well as I should, the fault is mine and not theirs.

Even if the other person is wrong or difficult to deal with, it's pretty hard to change them. We can, however, improve the way we act, talk, or even think about a situation. A hunting buddy of mine, Evangelist Richard Bailey, asked his wife one night to tell him all the little things about him that she didn't like or that bothered her. He wanted to change those things and make her happier. Several hours later, he asked if he could go to sleep and continue the conversation the next day. Richard challenged me to ask Chris that same question, but I'm not sure I have the time or the courage to hear her answers.

Jesus has instructed us to examine ourselves to be better husbands, wives, friends, and Christians. We need to do this often, and we need to look at our shortcomings openly, much like looking at that stump when the water level is low. After all, that's how God sees us—He looks right into our hearts.

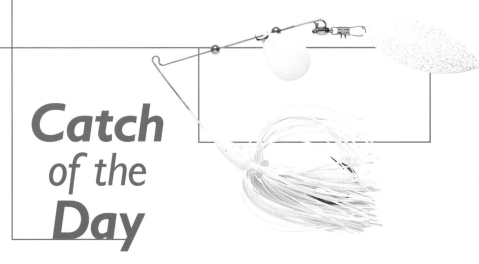

Catch
of the
Day

The only way we can build on or maintain healthy relationships is by pulling away the facade and all the things that hide the real person underneath.

When we expose our true inner person, our loved ones learn to love the real us. That is who God really wants us to be.

Because of His love for us and the love that other folks give to us, our shortcomings and faults can be turned into strengths. Love truly can bring forgiveness, restoration, or reformation in each of our lives.

> *And above all things have fervent love for one another, for "love will cover a multitude of sins."*
>
> I PETER 4:8

Those who love us are more willing to stand beside us when we are open enough to let them see who we really are. They just want us to be honest. Then even our weaknesses can be covered with love and forgiveness.

Chapter 9

Grass

Most of all lakes in the North and a fairly good number in the South have a natural element that's a fisherman's dream—grass!

Not only is grass a great place to fish, but it also can turn a lake into a great fishery. When grass is present, the bass will flourish, and bluegill, crappie, shad, and even waterfowl will be more abundant and healthy. To many dock owners or lakeside homeowners, grass can be a nuisance. To the sportsman, however, grass is a true blessing.

Without a doubt, the single most important thing to remember when fishing grass is to fish the edges—the inside or outside edge or even the edges of a hole in the grass. Where that edge forms a point or an indentation is usually the best fishing. If you can actually see the edge, it's fairly easy to cast to the right spot. If not, you'll need a good locator. Most pros would rather use a flasher in the grass, which is what I prefer.

Lots of baits work well in grass. My favorites are a Terminator spinnerbait and a Rebel Pop R. The spinnerbait can be fished in shallow grass as well as deep. In fact, one of the best ways to catch bass in deep grass is by slow-rolling a $^3/_4$ to 1 ounce Terminator. I like chartreuse and blue or white, and I use a willow leaf most frequently. I also usually add a plastic trailer to the spinnerbait.

If you can't locate the edges or even many times when you can, a Cordell Hot Spot is a great choice in a shad color. I like blue and chrome or purple and chrome. If you've got to fish through and under the grass, a black/blue/purple jig or a Texas-rigged worm with a straight tail in a darker opaque color would be my choice.

Grass is a blessing to fishermen, but so is everything we enjoy on God's earth. So much of what God blesses us with we take for granted. It's so easy for a Christian, or even a non-Christian, to thank God for a great miracle, but we can thank him for even our next breath.

What does God want in return for these great and small miracles? When Jesus healed the lame man at the pool at Bethesda, Jesus charged him to stop sinning; if he didn't, Jesus warned that something worse would happen to him. Now that should grab our attention! Jesus didn't say that He would cripple the man again or that He would do something worse to the man. Instead, his choices would determine what would happen to him for eternity.

As a Christian, our sins are covered by the blood of Jesus. When we confess and ask for forgiveness, our sins are remembered no more. When we keep sinning, something worse might happen. Jesus sanctifies, but sin creates consequences. As we accept God's blessings, we need to remember that Jesus commanded, "Stop sinning!"

Catch of the Day

We often believe that because of our sinful nature and our weaknesses, a certain amount of sinning can continue to go on in our lives. But we have a power source that can enable us to stay out of much of sin's grasp.

Jesus came to save. He gave us the ability to refrain from sin, and He sent His Spirit to guide us into truth. He taught that He would indwell believers by His Spirit and teach us how to live better lives.

> He who is in you is greater than he who is in the world.
>
> I JOHN 4:4

Scripture says, "Resist the devil and he will flee from you" (James 4:7). We need to believe that we can stand in His power and resist temptations that come along.

Chapter 10

Boat Docks

The first fishing tournament I ever won was on Lake Fort Gibson in eastern Oklahoma. I was twenty-two years old and a senior in college. It was a preliminary round for the Oklahoma State Championship.

The following year, I entered the same tournament on Fort Gibson, but I was having a really tough day. I'd spent the morning fishing isolated stumps in Jane Dennis and Clear Creeks but had only two small keepers. At about noon, I pulled into the Snug Harbor Cove to fish the floating docks. Using a $1/4$ ounce purple Redman spinnerbait with a single copper Colorado blade, I quickly pulled a limit out from under the docks. The very last dock, the one closest to the mouth of the cove, produced the winner. As I paralleled the side of the dock with the spinnerbait just below the bottom of floating barrels, a six-and-a-half pounder cruised out and inhaled the bait. First place and big bass that day taught me a lot about floating docks and helped instill one of my primary beliefs—never give up!

A few points about docks will help you catch those fish lurking underneath. First, remember that if you catch a fish from under a dock, there are usually more in the same place or more under nearby docks. Second, any dock that is by itself is usually a better site than a string of docks close together. Third, the older the dock and the trashier it is, the better. Fourth, docks on or near a point should never be overlooked, and the bigger bass will generally be under the dock closest to the main lake.

The time of the year and the weather may vary these principles a bit, but more often than not, these are some pretty good rules to follow. In May, I still prefer a spinnerbait with docks. In the fall—late September, October, and November—my choice is a Heddon Zara Spook. This bait will really pull some giants out from under the docks.

Faith in these lures and these principles comes from tournament success like that day over thirty years ago on Lake Fort Gibson. Faith in God and God's principles are built on an everyday relationship with Him.

Faith is the "evidence of things not seen" (Heb. 11:1). We usually can't see the bass under the floating dock, but because of what we know about how to fish docks, we have faith that the bass are there, thus increasing our hope to catch one. Though we can't see God (and we are a couple of thousand years too late to see Jesus), we can see all that God has created. We can see Him work for us and with us in our daily struggles.

We increase our faith every time a bass cruises out and strikes our bait. Likewise, we certainly should increase our faith every day as we see God at work around and in us. If your faith is lacking a bit or if you can't see God at work in your life, it's time to draw closer to God. A little lack of faith is nothing to be ashamed of. Even Jesus' closest disciples had "little faith" at times.

Catch of the Day

Some people want to be able to see around the bends of life, to know everything that is going to happen. But that's not faith. Scripture even says that's sin.

A friend of mine gave me a great quote about faith: "Faith is seeing what is not so as if it were so, and trusting God to make it so."

If we believe God loves us and has our best interest at heart, then we should believe that He will take care of our every step. We don't have to see around the bend because we know that He is watching out for us. We only need to continue walking as He taught us and believe that He will bless us in all things.

> For we walk
> by faith,
> not by sight.
>
> 2 CORINTHIANS 5:7

Faith steps in to allow you to live with confidence in the "author and finisher of our faith": Jesus Christ.

Chapter 11
Stickups

When some folks hear the word *stickup*, they conjure up images of the old Wild West, of masked bandits riding into town on horseback and robbing banks or siding up beside stagecoaches to rob the people inside. I have never heard many bass fisherman tell the bass to "Come out with your hands up; I've got you covered."

A stickup to a fisherman is any single piece of wood that sticks up out of the water. It might be growing up from the bottom, such as a tiny tree, or it could be just a small limb stuck between a couple of rocks. A stickup is different from a log, stump, brushpile, or even a regular tree; it's simply a stick that most people might not even notice. Remember, if a bass can get his eyes behind it, then the stickup is big enough to hold him for awhile. It's amazing how a bass will sometimes bypass all sorts of greatlooking cover to set up on a stickup. Sometimes, of course, there's a big old brushpile under that tiny stick.

Stickups are pretty easy to fish. I prefer a titanium spinnerbait or plastic worm most of the time, but a lot of baits can catch fish in these spots. You'll probably want to use a little longer cast than you would on a log or stump. Even with a worm, it's usually better to throw past a stickup and bring your bait to the fish. As with most cover, the more isolated the stickup, the better, and for some reason, multiple casts seem to be

needed. It's also important to wear sunglasses. There just might be a lot more structure under the water that you can't see without sunglasses.

Amazingly, these small structures quite often hold some of the biggest bass. Similarly, small faults and sins in our lives can and often do lead to some of our biggest problems. Little white lies, keeping the incorrect change from a sales clerk, harboring anger, or secretly coveting—these "little" sins seem insignificant when we commit them, but they can grow into huge problems and, of course, bigger sins. An unkind word, a hateful remark, or spreading gossip can inflict more damage than we could ever imagine and surely more than we intended.

How about fantasies and lust in your heart? No harm done most of the time, but this is just what the devil is looking for so that he can exploit it. He takes a sin and nurtures it and makes it grow until it literally can destroy families, marriages, and other relationships. Nowhere in the Bible do I find where God classifies any sin as big or small. Maybe that's because what we call "small sins" can be just as damaging as the big ones.

Catch
of the
Day

As Christians, we all know when something isn't quite right in our lives. We know it by that little nagging "something" that won't leave us alone. That's the Holy Spirit attempting to remind us of sin we haven't properly dealt with.

However, if we ignore that "feeling" or reminder, we can grow colder or more insensitive to God's influence in our lives. The longer we hold on to that sin, the easier it is to commit more sins and lessen God's influence on us.

> *If I regard iniquity in my heart, the Lord will not hear.*
>
> PSALM 66:18

The Psalmist understood about holding on to sin. He realized his entire relationship with God suffered when he refused to deal with personal issues.

Remember, over two-thirds of an iceberg is never seen. When we have unconfessed sins in our lives, there may be more hiding below the surface. But the Bible says, "If we confess our sins, He is faithful and just to forgive us our sins" (1 John 1:9).

Chapter 12

Brushpiles

Summertime fishing on my home lake, Tenkiller, in eastern Oklahoma, means fishing brushpiles. We have literally thousands of pieces of brush all over the lake. Bass and crappie fishermen have placed these super structures in Tenkiller, ranging in depth from just a few feet to forty to fifty feet. On a lake like Tenkiller and many others in the South, all you need is a good locator to find a bunch of these fish producers.

To find a brushpile, pay attention to the bank. If you find a place where trees have been cut down, you can count on a brushpile being nearby in the lake. Look in all the usual places—points, drops, ledges, humps, and so on. Most fishermen will place this brush in a spot that is already a home to fish. Around just about any dock, you'll find a brushpile or two about a cast distance away from the dock. These are the private hot spots for the dock owner.

A key thing to remember about a brushpile is that there is usually more brush down there than you think. You may only feel your bait bump the brush a time or two but believe me—and don't be fooled—I've placed huge willow trees and sycamores in the water that you can hardly feel with a lure.

A Texas rigged worm is my favorite for brushpiles. The deeper the water, the heavier the slip sinker. This is one time when you can fish with heavy

line, 17 to 25 pound test. Also, the deeper the water, the bigger the worm. Ten-inch plastic worms will be on my rods most of the time in these deep brushpiles. How about a secret color? Tomato red!

In order to fish a brushpile correctly, you need the right equipment. A cane pole and a bobber will catch a lot of fish, but it won't do you much good in a twenty-foot deep brushpile. As Christians, we also need the right equipment so that we can take a stand against the devil's schemes. Our armor includes traits like truth, righteousness, faith, and peace.

Peace is something we desire in life, but it is impossible to attain on our own. In Ephesians, we read that peace is from God. It is attained by being close to our Lord and being secure in our salvation. This allows us to face the everyday struggles of jobs, relationships, finances, and illness.

Peace allows us to forgive and forget when we are wronged—even when we are wronged by those we love the most. Peace like a river that floods our soul—that's what God gives. No matter what is done

to us, or what is said about us, or how bad a day we may be having, God's peace will over-whelm us. When we put on peace as part of our equipment, problems will roll off of us like water off a Gore-Tex rainsuit.

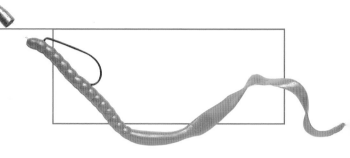

Catch of the **Day**

*J*esus offered peace to those who would trust Him, not a temporary or fleeting peace but permanent peace that comes only from God.

This peace gives a calm assurance that God is in control of every situation. It allows us not to be shaken by the news of the day. In a world that becomes more chaotic and rebellious all of the time, peace is something most folks only dream about.

Peace is available to everyone. It's a great offer! But only those who are willing to trust Jesus Christ can truly claim it. Do you know peace like the world offers it, or do you know the true lasting peace that Jesus gives?

> The peace of God, which surpasses all understanding, will guard your hearts and minds through Christ Jesus.
>
> PHILIPPIANS 4:7

Chapter 13

Reeds

While taping an ESPN show recently near Tarpon Springs, Florida, I had a great day catching bass around reeds. I was fishing with Ben Johnson, the inventor and one of the owners of Terminator spinnerbaits. We were fishing the reeds using two different techniques on spinnerbaits. Ben was letting his Terminator fall as close as possible near the surface in order to get "strike shots" for television, and he was wearing me out all morning. He also had another advantage: a chartreuse and white silichrome skirt.

I was convinced that as the water warmed up, the bass would hit the bait just as well on top, and to be honest, I thought my chartreuse/blue/white skirt would catch just as many fish. Hours went by—I was correct on the technique, but dead wrong on the color. Through much searching, I found one more chartreuse and white silichrome skirt in the boat. Like magic, now both Ben and I were catching fish. For the day, Ben caught more fish, but I did manage to coax a giant bass that weighed over ten pounds to grab my Terminator off the top. That big ole girl was a pretty good kisser!

The key to catching fish around reeds are depth and junction areas. It's necessary to concentrate on points and cuts in the reeds. You also should always be on the lookout for opportunities to fish behind the

reeds. Under almost all circumstances, if deep water is close to the reeds, you will catch bigger bass. As the water warms up, topwaters, like a Rebel PopR, are super. You need to let them lie still before you start your retrieve. This gives a bass a little extra time to ease out of the reeds. Then that first movement sometimes produces a strike.

I believe most of us would be better off if we would spend a little extra time everyday alone with God. This might be through meditation, prayer, or reading God's Word. It could mean just being by yourself and visiting with Jesus as a friend.

Outdoorsmen might choose to spend time with God in a boat or in the woods. It doesn't matter too much where as it does how often we do

it. This should not be a time of petition where we simply ask God to grant our wishes. It needs to be a time of sharing your heart and soul. A time of thanking God for His leadership in your life.

Plan that extra time every day. You just might be amazed at what God has in store for you, and He's just waiting for you to find out.

Catch
of the
Day

The Psalmist, David, understood our great need for time with God. He was determined to seek God in the morning, during the day, and in the evening. More than anything, David wanted to seek God's face and enjoy His fellowship.

Praying shouldn't always be about asking and receiving; it should focus on enjoying the company of God. And what a blessing that can be—to know that we can walk directly into God's throne room in prayer and spend time there with Him.

Evening and morning and at noon I will pray, and cry aloud, and He shall hear my voice.

PSALM 55:17

Some of life's most enjoyable times can be found in simply sitting with someone you love and who loves you. The believer's life is richly blessed by being in the presence of the Lord God Almighty who loves us more than anything.

Chapter 14

Lily Pads

In our early days of tournament fishing, Chris and I thought that just about every piece of water was new and exciting. Every lake contained a different structure to figure out. We first fished the Ross Barnett Reservoir near Jackson, Mississippi, in 1979 and '80. It was unlike any place we had ever fished, and it had something new—lily pads! Lily pads as big as dinner plates and as small as silver dollars.

Lily pads have a built-in location value if they are near a drop-off with deeper water close by. Because of the shade and the great way pads hold baitfish, this is a serious place to fish. Although many bass are way back in the pads, most of my fish are on the edge of the pads or just a foot or two back. Since this is where I catch most of the fish, I don't spend much time fishing too far back in the pads.

We catch a lot of bass by flipping a plastic worm or jig in the pads, but probably the best and most fun bait to use is a rubber frog. You'll want to pause the frog in any opening in the pads, no matter how small. Other than these pauses, a steady retrieve works fairly well. Green is a good color, but white is my favorite.

To fish these pads, you'll need a large dose of discipline. You very seldom will catch a bass on the initial strike. If you set the hook when you see the blow-up, you may never catch one all day. Wait, wait, wait, and still wait until you feel the fish before you set the hook. If you jerk and miss,

get that frog back in the hole as quickly as possible. You can also chunk a worm back in the hole created by the bass.

Unfortunately, patience is a key ingredient missing in a lot of folks lives in today's world. This is due to a lack of discipline that has permeated our society, and it has wrecked a lot of our moral and ethical values.

Discipline must begin almost at birth. We all know that any child will get away with as much as he or she can. In too many homes, even Christian homes, there are no limits. As we allow undisciplined behavior to continue in our children, evil actually grows in their hearts. Kids who kill kids, join gangs, steal and tell lies are all glaring examples. These, however, are only the tip of the problem. Undisciplined kids eventually grow into undisciplined adults who create a whole new set of problems

for themselves and those around them.

God requires discipline in our lives. Raising a child in church helps instill God's discipline in that young mind and heart. The reward is great if we teach our children this strength that will build values instead of compromising them.

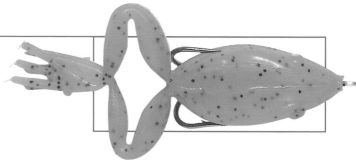

Catch of the **Day**

God talks a lot about teaching and training when it comes to children. We are admonished to provide a godly example and strong leadership for our families to follow.

God expects us to set boundaries and parameters in our children's lives. Proverbs 29:15 says, "A child left to himself brings shame to his mother."

> *Train up a child in the way he should go, and when he is old he will not depart from it.*
>
> PROVERBS 22:6

We have all seen the unfortunate results of children who were not given godly discipline. But by the same token, God as our Father has set certain parameters and guides for every believer to follow. Some may feel the teachings of the Bible are too rigid or confining. However, God only says "no" to things that will harm His children.

He expects us to live life to its fullest and have a great time, but He also sets boundaries that He expects us to honor and respect. That requires discipline to listen and obey His teachings in any situation.

Chapter 15

Glop

Glop. There's a term you haven't seen in too many fishing books. I'm not really too sure where the word came from, but it refers to the mixture of algae and vegetation that grows on the surface of a lot of our lakes, principally natural or God-made lakes. Lakes in Florida, the southern coast lakes, far northern lakes, and most of the delta-type waters have this glop. It's pretty messy to fish, but when the bass are in it, it's dyn-O-mite!

It's pretty much impossible to fish a bait under glop, so we need to use baits that work on top of it. My choices would be a silver spoon, a rubber frog, or a plastic worm. I like the spoon best. Depending on the time of the year and the baitfish, I'll dress the spoon with a skirt or a plastic trailer. If you notice bluegill feeding in the glop or hear the "pop" of their jaws feeding under the glop, a yellow and black skirt seems to work best. Another great skirt color is a chartreuse/lime/red combination.

The technique is simple. Throw the spoon out on top of the glop and wind it back in with a medium to slow steady retrieve. The bait will leave trails on top of the cover. Space your next cast three or four feet from your last trail and wind it in. Any brush, wood, or other hard cover demands an extra cast or two. This is definitely one type of topwater fishing that creates a lot of missed strikes. The great thing about these missed hits is you have a trail to follow and a hole in the glop that will let you know where the bass are located. Repeat that cast and your odds will increase greatly on your next strike!

Just as that spoon leaves trails in the glop, we leave trails every day in all that we do. Every action we take, every word we speak, no matter how careless or thoughtless, has an impact on someone. We obviously can leave trails of happiness and joy with those we meet. Sometimes nothing more than a cheerful smile can help brighten another person's day.

Even in the most painful times of Jesus' life, His concern was for others. The trails we leave each day will depend on where our concern is. Amazingly, when our concern turns to those around us, our day becomes better. Our attitude becomes brighter. Our problems become smaller. How would the world be changed if every Christian determined to leave happy trails every day? Those late airplanes, grouchy clerks, rude drivers, and inconsiderate friends and family members wouldn't really bother us so much at all. In fact, our trails of joy just might create a little joy somewhere we least expect it. When you leave a happy trail, keep repeating that cast day after day.

Catch of the **Day**

A story is told of the fellow who visited a local church that was cold, formal, and stodgy. During the singing part of the service, the old fellow was laughing and singing loudly and having a great time.

One of the ushers approached him and told him that he'd have to quiet down or leave. The old timer replied, "Sir, I've got the joy of the Lord." To which the usher responded, "Well, you didn't get it here, so hold it down."

> *Rejoice in the*
> *Lord always.*
> *Again I will*
> *say, rejoice!*
>
> PHILIPPIANS 4:4

If someone is happier or more excited about life than we are, we call them a fanatic. If they are depressed and discouraged, we call them realistic. Whenever Jesus came to a city and shared His ministry, there was always joy and celebration when He left. People were healed, a few were resurrected, many sins were forgiven, and many souls were saved. Why not choose to spread His joy around?

Chapter 16

Fine-Tuning
a Jerkbait

Jerkbaits may just be the best minnow imitators ever developed in hard plastics. Rogues, Redfins, Rebel minnows and the like are in everyone's tackle box, and they all have teeth marks on them. It doesn't matter if you have a lot of skill with jerkbaits or if you're just starting to use them; in either case, you can catch fish—all kinds of fish: bass, pike, crappie, even catfish. A close friend of mine, Jeff Fletcher, just caught a 64 pound, 8 ounce freshwater striper on a Rogue—and he was fishing for white bass!

Without a doubt, the secret to a jerkbait is to make sure it runs straight. Throw it out, and wind it in fast. If it goes to the right or left, you've got to "fine-tune" it. There are two ways to do this. One is with needlenose pliers—gently bend the line-tie in the opposite direction the bait is running. The second is with a sharp pocketknife—carefully shave the side of the bill opposite to the way it runs. If it runs to the left, shave the right side. Both of these methods equalize the water pressure on the bill of the lure, which makes the bait run straight.

You can catch fish with a jerkbait that doesn't run straight, but if it doesn't, you'll always sacrifice some depth. Quite often, the deeper you can get your jerkbait, the more fish you'll catch. The lighter the line you use, the deeper you'll be able to fish a jerkbait. A good all-around line

size is 10 pound test, but I'll use 6 and 8 pound a lot and sometimes as heavy as 14 pound.

I find that my walk with God needs to be fine-tuned frequently. The pressures of everyday living get me running a little crooked at times, making it really difficult to always walk the straight and narrow. I know that when I leave that straight path, I create problems for myself and those around me.

Probably the best way to fine-tune our lives is with prayer and by reading God's Word. The more I pray, the more God seems to lead my behavior and my thinking. God's Word is filled with instructions to direct everything we do. These instructions are meant to benefit us on a day-by-day basis. As long as we're doing the things that God loves and avoiding the practices God hates, our lives will run pretty smoothly.

When problems occur, the reason can be found in our walk with God getting a little off-center. The further we stray from God's instructions, the bigger the problems become. We are so fortunate we serve a God who not only can solve our problems but also waits patiently while we make our mistakes. Even while we are falling short of God's standards, He is already at work bringing us back to Him.

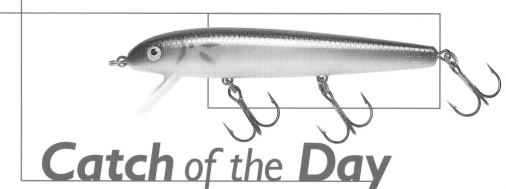

Catch of the Day

Many of us are familiar with the story of the prodigal son, who left home with his inheritance and then foolishly lost all he had (Luke 15). But do we understand the tremendous faithfulness of the father? The father knew his son shouldn't leave home, but he allowed it. The father probably also understood the hardships his son would endure, but he permitted his son to make his own choices. The greatest part of this father is that he also knew he would be faithful to his son no matter what. He was faithful, I believe, to pray for his boy. He was faithful to love his son unconditionally. And finally, he was faithful to accept and receive him home again.

> *For this my son was dead and is alive again . . .*
>
> LUKE 15:24

God is represented in the story by the father. Even when He knows we will stumble and falter and fail, He allows us to try our own way. He then is faithful to love us and call us back to Him.

Chapter 17
A Long Pause

It's pretty much accepted that the best way to work a jerkbait or a crankbait is with some sort of "stop and go" retrieve. That pause seems to come almost naturally with a jerkbait, but it is harder to remember when fishing with a crankbait. With the advent of suspending baits, a whole new world of opportunities opened up to fishermen in determining how long to let that bait lie still. A general rule of thumb is the colder the water, the longer the pause. Since a suspended bait won't rise back to the surface, we can leave it out there as long as we want.

At a B.A.S.S. tournament on Wilson Lake in Alabama, I caught a couple of big limits on a Rogue. The water temperature was in the fifty-degree range, and it took an extra long pause to trigger a strike. In fact, almost every hit came just about the time I was ready to give up and jerk the bait again.

Remember that the more aggressive the bass are, the shorter the pause you'll need. Most of us are pretty impatient and don't let the bait sit still long enough. If you're fishing these baits and not having much success, it's a pretty good bet that you'll need to pause the bait a little longer. The tougher the fishing, the longer the pause.

You might want to start out working the bait pretty fast and then gradually make your stops a little longer until you start getting strikes. When you stop the bait, move your rod tip toward the bait, creating a little slack in the line. This will allow your lure to suspend more naturally and will

look a little more enticing to the fish. It's vitally important to have extra sharp hooks because a bass is pretty much hooking itself when it strikes on the pause. Your next jerk on the lure is often just the follow-through on the hooks.

Pauses in our lives are important to God. He wants us to pause and rest daily. One of my biggest struggles is with my overflowing schedule and lack of time. I need rest!

When Jesus' disciples returned from a missionary journey, He asked them to go with Him to "a deserted place and rest a while" (Mark 6:31). Not only do we need to rest, but we need to go with Jesus to a quiet place. It's easy for me to rest close to Jesus as I look out an airplane window, or across a lake, or into a patch of beautiful woods. An outdoorsman lives in God's creation every time he hunts or fishes.

A lot of successful Christians set aside a period of quiet to be with Jesus every day. It could be in a boat, an office, a bedroom, or a car. This rest with Jesus lets us slow down and focus on all that He has done and is doing in our lives. It gives our emotions a chance to run at a more manageable speed. This brings us closer to God and makes us more like Jesus.

Catch of the *Day*

*T*he Scriptures tell us that we can know God better when we are still. I don't think this means we have to be motionless. Instead, there are times we must allow Him to speak to us in quiet. We must put ourselves in a state of calmness in order to learn about Him.

Samuel, the young prophet, heard God's voice on three occasions, but he didn't know who was speaking to him. That probably describes most of us. If God called to us, we probably wouldn't know it was Him.

If we include God in our lives on a regular basis, He will speak to us. Are you listening?

> Be still,
> and know
> that I
> am God.
>
> PSALM 46:10

Chapter 18

Pumping a Spot

One of the easiest of all baits to catch fish on is a Cordell Hot Spot. This bait is shaped like a baitfish, is filled with rattles, and comes in just about every color imaginable. Although it's a great bait for your first day of bass fishing, you'll find plenty of them in every pro's tackle box. I have at least one tied on almost all the time. Most fish are taken on this lure by just chunkin' and windin'. Throw it out, and reel it in—fast or slow. Almost anything works.

One of my tricks with this bait is to pump the Spot. I do this with a controlled fall on a tight line. You need to keep the Spot straight or level as it falls. As your rod tip gets close to the water, simply sweep it up at a speed fast enough to feel the Spot vibrate. Then repeat the controlled fall. I'll normally only use two to four pumps per cast. After the pumps, just lower your rod tip and crank it in. Most of your strikes will come on the controlled fall. This technique really works well on points or on the edges of grasslines.

When you're fishing a Hot Spot, or "pull bait" as the pros call them, it's best to use a heavier action rod than you might normally use for crankbaits. I like a six-and-a-half foot medium-heavy Jimmy Houston Signature Series Shimano rod. This heavier action allows you to get the hooks into the fish a lot better. If you use a softer rod on these baits, you will see a lot of bass throw your bait.

Control of the bait is the key to being able to pump a Spot correctly. Control seems to be something we all want in our lives as well. We want to be able to control what happens to us, but so much that affects us is out of our control. And much of what we can control, we don't manage very well.

Part of God's plan of salvation includes giving Him control of our lives. This is one of the hardest parts of our walk with God. Too often, I try to do God's work for Him. I forget that God is in the problem-solving business. He knows our strengths and how to use them. He also knows our weaknesses and how to use them. Most importantly, He knows our weaknesses and how to strengthen them.

When we give God the control that He wants and deserves, we don't need to worry about the results. God doesn't make mistakes like I do. His decisions, His leadership, and His principles are always right. Remember, He has the resources of the whole world at His fingertips!

Catch of the Day

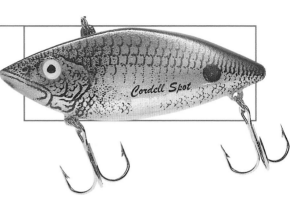

Cordell Spot

*T*he imagery in 2 Timothy 1:12 is similar to a bank deposit. When we make a deposit at the bank, we feel confident that we have placed our money in a safe place. In like manner, when we receive salvation, we entrust our eternity with God Himself. Our salvation is not dependent upon our good deeds, and the safekeeping of our soul is not dependent upon anyone or anything other than the greatness of God.

> *He is able to keep what I have committed to Him until that Day.*
>
> 2 TIMOTHY 1:12

If we had anything to do with attaining salvation, then we could do something to cause us to lose it. But since God's grace enabled it, God's Son purchased it, and God's Spirit explained it—all we can do is accept it.

My salvation wasn't provided by me; therefore, it's not kept by me. And like Paul, I can say that what I committed to Him until judgment is in His safekeeping.

Chapter 19

Weighting Baits

Today, most bait manufacturers build suspended crankbaits and jerkbaits, so you don't hear nearly as much about adding weights to lures. But weights are still needed sometimes when you want to suspend that special bait. The quickest and easiest way to add weight is to wrap lead strips around the shank of the trebles. If you don't have the lead strips, you can use a split-shot sinker. This is quick, and you can easily remove the lead to stop the suspension.

Storm builds two products called SuspenStrips and SuspenDots that are handy to have in your tackle box. These can be added to the underneath or the sides of a bait. They're self-adhesive, and on some larger lures, can even be put on the bill. If you have the time, it's best to test the baits in a sink, tub, or pool. I want the suspended baits to sit level or to float with the nose pointed slightly downward.

Spinnerbaits can also work well with added weight, especially very small spinnerbaits. If you need a small bait (⅛ to ³⁄₁₆ ounce) when fishing, you might have some difficulty casting it, particularly if it's windy or if you're looking for pinpoint accuracy. A lead strip or split shot can make a world of difference. You can add the lead to the wire frame, but I like to attach it to the hook underneath the skirt. This hides the lead and keeps the

same profile, yet it gives me a more manageable spinnerbait. I also do this in smallmouth waters when I'm trying to get more distance on a $^3/_8$ or $^1/_2$ ounce bait.

Added weight to a lure can make fishing more exciting, but added weight in our daily struggles can seem unbearable. Sometimes it feels like the whole world is against us. Even those we love most can say and do things that add to our problems. On these days, we have an important choice to make. We can either have our own little "pity party" and feel sorry for ourselves, or we can turn to Jesus and read His words on the situation.

Remember Jesus' last night with His disciples? He told them, "These things I have spoken to you, that in Me you may have peace. In the world you will have tribulation; but be of good cheer, I have overcome the world" (John 16:33). This means that we can place the weight of our troubles on Jesus. We don't need to worry or even try to bear it on our own. Jesus has overcome the world and all of our problems with it. Jesus

did this so that we might have peace. He knew we would have troubles, but through it all, we need to take heart and live within God's peace. Then, we can stay positive, no matter how heavy our burdens are. We have the strength of God to carry them.

Catch of the **Day**

In the Scriptures, Jesus often used simple illustrations from life to make His point. He said we should take His yoke because it is easy and His burden is light. He used this farming image to explain salvation to His listeners at that time. His illustration explains that one ox alone cannot effectively pull the plow to do the work that is needed in the field. But when two are harnessed together, they can share the burden and the plowing responsibilities. Then when one ox becomes a little weary, the second ox takes more of the load.

The load becomes lighter when it can be shared. In our lives, Jesus offers a yoke with Him that will ease our burdens and lighten our load. He offers to share our troubles and our sorrows. He says that He will take the extra weight if we will shift it to Him.

> *Take My yoke upon you and learn from Me, for I am gentle and lowly in heart, and you will find rest for your souls. For My yoke is easy and My burden is light.*
>
> MATTHEW 11:29–30

Chapter 20

Deep in the Heart

For years, one of my basic principles in bass fishing has been to fish the heaviest cover possible, no matter what it turned out to be, but this can be difficult when you encounter water that has an abundance of cover. In heavy cover, you often think that you can catch a fish on every cast, but after a couple of hours of throwing baits at beautiful spots and not catching anything, it's natural to think that the fish are just not biting. That could be true, but most likely, the bass have a small strike zone and are just not willing to move very far to take your bait.

Generally, when the fish are acting this way, they'll also move to the meanest, thickest part of the cover. This is when you need to use baits and tactics that will get you deep into the heart of the cover. The technique that works best in this situation is flipping. The bait I like best is a jig in a ³/₈ to ³/₄ ounce size. The thicker the cover, the heavier the jig, and I use a pork chunk or plastic crawfish trailer. As the water warms up, I'll switch over to a Texas-rigged lizard, worm, or craw. Under most situations, the bass will sit in the cover and not on the bottom, so pay extra attention to your bait as it falls. You'll get most strikes on the initial drop.

In the heart of heavy cover, you'll find a great catch. In the heart of every person, God searches for purity. He knows the desires of our hearts. He also knows the evil that may be lurking there, such as greed, jealousy,

envy, hatred, sexual immorality, and much more. It is important to step back and take a close look at what we have deep in our hearts and determine what needs to be changed—even those things we're ashamed of and don't want to share with others.

Keep in mind that God has equipped His followers with the ability to overcome this evil. I constantly pray for a pure heart, knowing I can't be the kind of man my family and friends deserve if I have sin inside of me. This seems to be one of the ways the devil likes to operate from the inside out.

If he can grow any of these evils in us, we'll eventually bring them to the surface and act upon them. When we do, it's a victory for Satan.

God has given us His Holy Spirit to help us remove the sin in our hearts. He makes sure we recognize that sin for what it is and what it can do to us. We can then turn the problem over to God through prayer, which will purify our hearts.

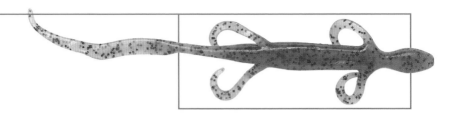

Catch *of the* **Day**

Satan uses any unconfessed sin to hurt me and damage my relationship with God. Sin must be seen for what it is. It must be viewed as God views it. It must not be tolerated.

The writer of Hebrews said we should "lay aside every weight, and the sin which so easily ensnares us" (12:1). Just as a runner strips off any extra weight in order to run his fastest, believers must be willing to cast off things that can hinder our race for Christ.

> *For out of the abundance of the heart his mouth speaks.*
>
> LUKE 6:45

The Bible also tells us that out of the hearts of men proceeds every other thought or deed. If we have sin stored in our lives, it's very easy for ill will, strife, and evil to come from our mouths. We generally get into trouble by not guarding our hearts and allowing things to lurk there that must be removed.

Chapter 21

Fish Your Strength

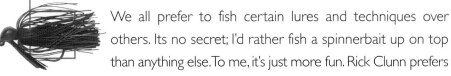 We all prefer to fish certain lures and techniques over others. Its no secret; I'd rather fish a spinnerbait up on top than anything else. To me, it's just more fun. Rick Clunn prefers a crankbait, Larry Nixon a lizard, Tommy Biffle a jig. I could go on and on. As with most top pros, these men can fish most lures and techniques extremely well, but when you see them in the winner's circle or near the top of the standing, you can bet they are fishing to their strength.

It is important to fish to your strength when the fish are biting. It's even more important to fish to strength when you're having trouble getting bites. When nothing seems to work, do what you do best. It might not seem like the best thing to do that day, but if it's what you do best, you're probably going to have some success. I can promise you—that's how the pros play it. It brings confidence.

In our Christian walk, we also have strengths given to us by God. The Bible calls these strengths the gifts of the Holy Spirit, and they are promised to every Christian. They include prophecy, teaching and preaching, exhortation, sharing, leading, and showing mercy as well as the gifts of performing miracles, healing, helping, administration, speaking in tongues, and cheerfulness. Our strengths blend together with the strengths of other Christians to do God's work.

My wife, Chris, has the gifts of exhortation and mercy. Her strength in exhortation allows her to comfort and encourage other Christians. It gives her the ability to lovingly minister to friends and family when they have needs. In showing mercy, she's uniquely equipped to be sensitive to those suffering from all kinds of problems. She's willing to give both her time and resources to help anytime and everywhere she can. Through so many of these situations, she shows a strength that can only come from God.

If we're saved, God has given us one or more of these great spiritual strengths. Through the good days and the bad, it's our duty to use that gift faithfully.

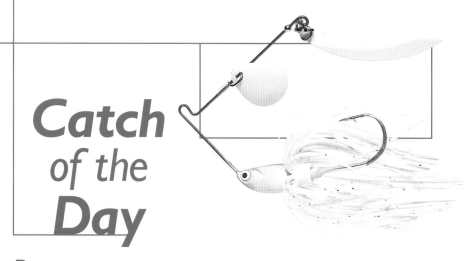

Catch
of the
Day

*P*aul wrote that there is a battle going on inside every believer. The flesh is at war with the Spirit. God intends for us to live life to its utmost, but He also seeks to show us the best way to do that. All of us have a choice: we can receive the best God has to offer or we can follow our own desires.

God tells us that following our flesh can lead to adultery, strife, lies, drunkenness, drugs, and violence. On the other hand, if we allow the Spirit to take over, our lives will be filled with the fruits of the Spirit, such as love, joy, peace, goodness, patience, and trust.

> *Walk in the Spirit, and you shall not fulfill the lust of the flesh.*
>
> GALATIANS 5:16

It seems simple to me that this is a war I don't want my flesh to win. So . . . Surrender! Give up your things for God's things.

Chapter 22

Changing Blades

Most spinnerbait companies build their baits with the same philosophy: match the blade to the size of the head. This keeps the bait running straight. So, the smaller the bait, the smaller the blade, and as the spinnerbait increases in size, the blade increases to match.

Most of the time, this philosophy works, but don't get locked in. On a windy day, you might need a small spinnerbait to catch fish, but since small baits don't throw well in the wind, you'll want to move up to a larger bait and change the blade(s) to a smaller size. This will allow you to make great casts with a small profile bait. You might also want to trim the skirt a bit and use a smaller trailer—or no trailer at all. Conversely, you might want to slow down the fall rate on a large spinnerbait. You'll need to do this quite early in the year when the water is colder. Changing to a large blade on a smaller bait is a great solution. A big blade on a $^3/_8$ ounce head will literally float down and produce a lot of strikes.

Outdoor Innovations recently developed the Jimmy Houston Tournament Speed Bead Series Terminators. These baits include our two latest inventions at Terminator. First, a speed bead that allows instant changing of the end blade on a spinnerbait. Second, a unique device that allows you to change the blade on the shaft. In the past, I've never been able to do these changes without tearing up the bait and rebuilding it. Now these quick

blade changes can be done on the water without losing much fishing time—and time is precious for a tournament fisherman.

Time is also precious in successfully raising a family. You can never spend too much time with your family. It's important to remember that what your kids see you doing has just as much influence as anything you say.

Chris and I have always included our kids in everything—work, play, and also church. They now do the same with their own kids, and we're seeing our grandchildren being raised the same way.

It's not always easy to include your family in what you do. It takes sacrifice, and it can be costly. As kids grow older, they may not want to

be included, but believe me, the closer you keep your family, the more blessed you will be.

As we fight for time with our family in this fast moving world, we need to place our families at the top of our priority list. If we exhibit godly values, we will develop godly families. That's what God intended when He created the family in the first place.

Catch
of the
Day

God created Adam and Eve, in His image, with a need to relate to Him and to one another. He then commanded them to multiply. His first order and plan was for families to be established and blessed.

Today, we often see families who don't relate to one another at all. Parents who don't exhibit love for one another are a common sight. Children are left to fend for themselves. But God's intention for families has not changed. He still intends for love to be shared in the home. He desires faithfulness and companionship to rule in our hearts.

> This is My commandment, that you love one another as I have loved you.
>
> 1 JOHN 15:12

Love, understanding, forgiveness, and compassion must be present in our homes if we hope to build true Christian families.

Chapter 23

Round
or Willow

 Blade configuration depends upon what you're trying to accomplish with your spinnerbait. The key points to remember are that round blades create more vibration and willow leaf blades create more flash. In dingy or muddy water, I like as much vibration as possible. Early in the year when we're trying to get bass to move longer distances to strike our bait, round blades are my preference.

My favorite round blade is an Oklahoma blade by Terminator—a deep-cut turtle back with the Terminator fishtail cut in the end of the blade. It vibrates more than any other round blade, and the fishtail cut gives it the elongated look of a willow leaf. It's the best combination of vibration and flash of any blade developed.

When you're fishing in clearer water and looking for more flash, willowleaf blades are your answer. Generally, I use a large willow leaf as my end blade with a smaller round Colorado blade on the shaft. If you've located fish in weeds or grass, a willow will fish much easier through this vegetation.

Tandem willow leaf blades have become popular, and they're one of my favorite baits. I particularly like this twin willow combo early in the year when the shad are spawning. This is a great bait for catching a really big bass. It seems that a chartreuse/blue spinnerbait with two large gold

willow blades produces more big bass for me every year than any other blade configuration. I don't know if this is because of the bait or the situations I fish it in. Most likely, it's a combination of the two.

We can create the best spinnerbait configuration for whatever fishing situation we're in, but we can't configure Christianity to fit into all of life's situations. We can't water down the principles and laws of God to fit into whatever makes us feel good. The laws of God haven't changed in thousands of years, yet many of us keep trying to place new interpretations on them.

Our beliefs must firmly be established on the principles of God rather than the principles of what folks say is politically correct. We can't indulge in a little gossip, a little backbiting, a little lying and cheating, or a little adultery and expect God to look at us and wink. No matter how much sugarcoating we allow society to put on sin, it's still sin, and the only interpretation that counts is God's.

I pray that God will always show me what is pleasing to Him in every situation. We're kidding ourselves as a nation, family, or as an individual when we believe we can achieve happiness and still violate God's principles.

Catch
of the
Day

When the Israelites were preparing to cross into the Promised Land, God appeared to their leader, Joshua, and gave His final instructions. He challenged Joshua to be strong, courageous, and bold. God particularly instructed Joshua to be obedient to the teachings of God. He was told to immerse himself in what the written law specified and not to vary or waver in his commitment to God's Word. If Joshua obeyed, then God promised to give him—and all of Israel—unprecedented favor.

Why do we sometimes seek every possible avenue for joy and success except the Lord's, when He already has a never-fail formula? His Word continues to be true to every generation. Success, joy, and prosperity will follow those who follow His teachings. As one old preacher said many years ago, "Someday someone will pick this Book up, read it, and live by it, and put the rest of us to shame."

> This Book of the Law shall not depart from your mouth...
>
> JOSHUA 1:8

Chapter 24

Lunkers

Everybody wants to catch big bass. One of the first questions asked among bass fishermen is, "What's the biggest bass you've ever caught?"

Catching giants sometimes happens by accident, but if you really want to land a big one, you've got to gear up for one. Probably the most important thing to remember is that big bass like big baits. These huge fish are accustomed to eating giant bluegill, large crappie, catfish, shad, and even other bass that weigh up to a pound or more. If you're fishing worms, use a ten to twelve inch in a large diameter. Dress a spinnerbait with a long bulky trailer, and use the biggest blades in your box. Follow the same rules with crankbaits and topwaters. Big Baits = Big Bass.

Also remember that these big bruisers won't work too hard to get a meal. This means you must slow down your presentation and make sure you work the structure as thoroughly as possible. Since the largest bass are females, this means they can be really finicky. Most of the time, you will need to take multiple casts to get her "in the mood" to strike. Your best time of the year to catch that "bass of a lifetime" is when she's most vulnerable—in the spring before she spawns. Your next best bet is in mid fall. If I were pressed to pick a magic depth, it would be ten feet, give or take a foot, depending on the time of year and type of lake I'm fishing.

A big bass is harder to catch because it is older and wiser. A small bass is prone to make more mistakes. As Christians, we are very much like

these bass. When we're young in our faith, we're easier prey for Satan. His best lures for the young are illicit sex or drugs. He uses these to tempt both men and women, single or married. God warns that these sins carry severe penalties, which may include disease, a broken marriage, and tremendous pain. Often it takes a lifetime of pain to pay for a few moments of so-called pleasure.

Pain is the devil's goal, and he will place incredible temptation in front of us to try to lead us into sin. He'll use peer pressure, alcohol, curiosity, or whatever it takes to hook us. He attacks a young Christian with more temptations than a non-believer. Christian or not, however, Satan will attack.

When we break God's rules, we will suffer the consequences every single time. Of course, God will forgive these sins, if we ask Him, just as He forgives every sin, small and large. When you find yourself in the midst of temptation, ask God to get you out of that situation immediately. The longer the devil can make you linger, the better chance he has to inflict pain.

Catch of the **Day**

Satan likes to make us feel like we're all alone. He tries to make us believe that no one else could withstand the temptation we're going through. However, Paul wrote that we all face similar temptations. We don't deal with anything new or unique or different than anyone else.

God has promised us that He will be faithful to us in the midst of every temptation. He won't allow us to go it alone, and He has promised us that He will not allow Satan to tempt us more than we can bear. Satan may seem like a "bad dog," but God always has him on a leash. In the midst of trials and temptations, Scripture says that God always will give us a way of escape.

> No temptation
> has overtaken you
> except such as is
> common to man.
>
> I CORINTHIANS 10:13

Please remember this important truth: God wants you to be successful in your walk. If you lean on and trust in Him, He won't allow Satan to pull you under with any temptation.

Others have faced your problem and won. So can you.

Chapter 25

Pitching

 I use both underhand casting and pitching as well as flipping. Pitching is the easiest to learn how to do. First, take your lure in your hand and strip off enough line so that your bait is between your reel and the first eye on your rod. With your button pushed on the reel and the bait in your hand, lower your rod tip. Now you're ready to pitch. Drop the bait, raise the rod . . . nothing to it.

With a little practice in your living room, backyard, or at the lake, you'll be pitching baits into spots that most folks could never cast into. Like all casting techniques, pitching is done with the wrist and not the arm. As with flipping and underhand casting, it is deadly accurate and can be extremely fast in covering water effectively.

The best pitching bait is a jig or Texas-rigged plastic worm. You can get by with a little smaller line with pitching than you can with flipping. This usually will give you a few more bites. You can also use a little shorter and lighter action rod, which lets you fish smaller or lighter baits, and it's more fun when you hook a fish. I pitch mostly with a six-and-a-half foot rod, but I flip with a seven or seven-and-a-half foot rod.

Some folks in our fast-paced society view Christianity as a pitch to reel in weak-minded and hurting people for other-than-godly reasons. They view television ministries as money-making schemes, churches as social

clubs, and Christians as self-righteous hypocrites who try to force their views on others. Though some people are guilty of all of the above, nothing could be further from these perceptions in real Christian circles.

God doesn't need our money. He owns everything already. And it is true that some churches are indeed social clubs, but most exist with one purpose: to preach Jesus in order to save people from hell and to teach the principles of serving God.

Every church has hypocrites, but if churches weren't full of sinners, we wouldn't need Jesus in the first place. The world needs Jesus; that is why Jesus came. When you have something of such great value, there will always be a few ready to exploit that value for some personal gain.

The real value and the real gain is felt by those who accept Jesus as their personal Lord and Savior and accept the pitch of the One who hung the moon and the stars. Literally.

Catch
of the
Day

In the day of Hezekiah, King of Israel, the people were vigorously worshipping the brass snake that Moses had made seven hundred years earlier. It was the same snake used by God to deliver the Israelites from the poisonous snake attack in the wilderness. This brass sepent was held in such high esteem that the Israelites revered it as a god. It had become an item of disgrace to God.

When Hezekiah came to the throne, he took the snake and broke it into pieces and called it "Nehushtan," which means "It is a piece of brass." He called it what it was and helped deliver the people from the curse of idolatry.

> Until those days the children of Israel burned incense to it, and called it Nehushtan.
>
> 2 KINGS 18:4

The Word of God has a habit of calling things as they really are. We must be willing to let the Word of God confront us with God's truth if we are to make any changes in our lives that will make us more like Jesus.

Chapter 26

Flipping

Flipping is a town in Arkansas where they build Ranger boats. It's also a deadly technique for catching bass. Some folks say pitching is merely flipping at a distance. The results you're looking for are the same with both techniques: a quiet and deadly accurate presentation into the thickest of all cover. But the mechanics you need to learn are entirely different.

Flipping first became popular some thirty years ago in California when my friend, Dee Thomas, became so skilled and so efficient at flipping that he was almost unbeatable in tournaments. Fortunately—or unfortunately—he shared his skills with the rest of us.

You'll want to learn to flip with a long rod—seven to seven-and-a-half feet—and you'll want to use heavy line, twenty pound test or higher with a good sized jig. A ⅝ ounce is probably best. Strip off about fifteen to eighteen feet of line and begin to swing the jig toward your target.

I think it's best to learn how to flip at home, in your living room or back-yard. The living room maybe the best because it will force you to lower your rod tip on the swing unless you have a pretty high ceiling. The biggest obstacle to learning is keeping your rod high and not lowering it on the swing. You must use your wrist and not your arm. The rod tip should lower almost to the ground or water and then raise to create the proper force to deliver your bait.

With practice, your delivery will become smooth and fluid. Another tip is to turn your off-rod hand (the one holding the line) to where it will allow the line to flow across your thumbnail and not your fingers.

Two other points to note: As soon as your bait hits the water, bring your off-rod hand to the rod. Now with both hands on the rod, you're ready to set the hook. Remember: flipping is a loose-line technique. When your bait enters the water, drop your rod tip and let the bait fall straight down on a loose line.

Just as Dee shared his flipping technique with others, we're commanded by God to share Jesus with those around us. Not only are we commanded, but God actually puts that desire into every Christian. The problem is that sometimes our desire is not as strong as our fear.

The Bible describes many examples of people who denied Jesus. The most prominent and well-known is Peter, who denied Jesus three times before the rooster crowed. We can deny Jesus not only with words or lack of words, but also by our actions.

I pray daily that others can see Jesus in me by the way I live and the words I speak, but frequently, they see and hear the devil instead. It's so comforting to see how Jesus forgave Peter and to read about Peter's ministry. I know that He's not through with me yet.

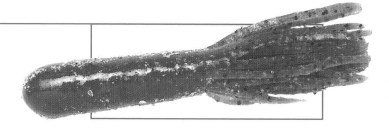

Catch of the *Day*

It's been said that what we truly care about shows up in our conversations and our pocketbooks. What invades our speech reveals what our heart is focused on—maybe it's our boat, our dog, our friends or grandkids. Also, what we spend our money on represents our favorite things—a fishing license, hunting trips, vacations with family, toys for the grandbaby.

If Jesus Christ is someone who is vitally important to you, don't you think He should also invade your thoughts, your conversation, and your billfold? Paul wrote that He was not ashamed of what Jesus had done in his life. Paul gave his life over to serving Christ day and night because of what Jesus had done for him.

> I am not ashamed of the gospel of Christ, for it is the power of God to salvation for everyone who believes.
>
> ROMANS 1:16

Chapter 27

Go Underhand

Developing and learning underhand casting has probably helped me more than any other technique. I developed it in my early days of tournament fishing in order to fish faster and cover more water. Still today, for tournament fishermen, it is essential.

Underhand casting will actually save about two seconds per throw. This doesn't sound like much, but a lot of our casts in bass fishing only take about ten seconds. Two seconds is 20 percent. Make 20 percent more casts in a tournament day and you'll catch a few more fish. Even with slower lures, a twenty-second cast can save 10 percent of your time, and 10 percent more casts equals more bass on the scales.

If time doesn't matter, you still can benefit greatly by changing overhand to underhand for accuracy reasons. I've never seen anyone who could throw as accurately overhanded as they could underhanded. In lure presentation, a key to getting more strikes is to make a quiet entry into the water with your bait. An underhand cast keeps your lure close to the water all the way out. It doesn't have far to fall, so you can gently raise your rod tip and ease your bait into the spot. This low flight path will let you throw under branches, limbs, boat docks, and places that you've never been able to get to before. If it's windy, your bait is going to be less affected by the wind, thus giving you both better lure presentation and accuracy.

With underhand casting, your hooksetting will improve because your rod will always be in a better hooksetting position when the bait hits the water. And if you're into family fishin' like I am and often fish with two or three or more folks in the boat, you're a lot less likely to hook each other.

While it's a great idea to cast underhanded, it's certainly not a way we want to live our lives. We often hear businesses and business people described as being "underhanded." We often characterize politicians and lawyers in this way. How did that come about? Probably from a compromise of principles.

This type of compromise in a person doesn't happen all at once. It's a slow erosion, much like waves washing away a bank. You don't notice much day-by-day, but after awhile, you see giant trees falling in the water—which is good for fishing but this erosion in our principles causes giant problems in our lives.

We constantly need to take a gut-check on what we believe and what we consider to be right and wrong. It's very easy to let our beliefs and values slide just a little in order to achieve a desired result. Then the

next time we face a similar situation, it's even easier to let it slide a little more. Pretty soon, we're doing and saying and thinking things that would have shocked us a few months or a few years back. We have eroded away what we first considered wrong.

It's difficult to fill in a bank that has been washed away. I often pray that I can build upon God's values and principles everyday and never be underhanded with anything or anybody.

Catch of the Day

When King David recognized his sin with Bathsheba, he cried out to God and asked to be allowed to enjoy God's salvation once again. He knew that his relationship with the Lord had been hurt because of his sins, but he also had an assurance that God had not discarded him. Yes, God was hurt and disappointed by the sins of this former shepherd boy, but David could lean on his personal relationship with God.

> *Restore to me the joy of Your salvation.*
>
> PSALM 51:12

In our lives, we often "mess things up" by compromising our principles. We then sin and make choices that obviously aren't in our best interest. But, just as in David's case, God doesn't cast us out of the family.

I feel great joy in knowing Christ as my Savior and understanding that God will never let go of me as His child. His grace and forgiveness extend far beyond anything I might do to offend His principles. I am His child!

Chapter 28

Practice for the Long Haul

The benefits of underhand casting are amazing. You can easily learn this technique by following two steps. First, create a loop or circle with your rod tip. The loop replaces the back-and-forth motion of an overhand cast, and it develops the power you'll need in the rod to cast the bait. Second, use a strong wrist. All casting is done with the wrist, not the arm. With your rod tip near the water, roll your wrist, creating a loop that is flat or parallel to the water. (This loop is similar to a Ferris wheel laid over on its side.) Your lure needs to be wound up all the way to the tip of the rod; then you can create the loop and snap your wrist up to make the cast. The loop builds the power, and the upward snap of your wrist delivers that power so that the lure shoots straight off your rod tip toward the target.

The absolute best way to learn this technique is to start overhand and work your way down. Keep your elbow in close to your side. This forces you to use your wrist. Drop your rod tip down three-fourths of the way; then move it directly out to your side.

Next, move the tip down near the water but still out to the side, which is where you'll feel your wrist automatically begin to turn or roll. Then, start exaggerating that roll until you've created a loop with the rod tip. At this point, you're throwing sidearm, which is a better cast than

overhand, but you know you've still got a little ways to go because the loop will be round and not parallel to the water.

Lastly, begin working the rod tip, starting from the side and then out in front of you. This last step is a little tricky, but it will flatten out the loop and will help you become proficient with the underhand cast. It takes practice, but it's worth it.

Practice is important in every part of our lives. We all need to accept and act on the challenge to practice what we preach.

It's difficult to keep our kids off drugs if we're drinking alcohol and smoking cigarettes. It's impossible to teach them honesty when they see us lying or bending the rules. How can our children learn about caring for others if we're not even caring for each other at home? We admonish children for being selfish—for not sharing with brothers,

sisters, and friends— but at the same time, we're sharing so little of our time or money with charities or the church. A lot of us are not even sharing much time with our own families. When we model godly behavior, our children have an example to follow into adulthood.

Catch
of the
Day

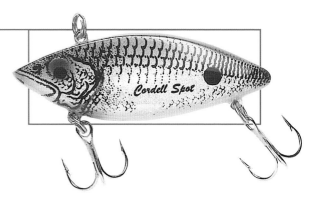

We live in a time when the world has exchanged truth for lies, right for wrong, love for lust, and holiness for happiness. In an age that seems so confused without a moral compass, what are we to do? How should we live?

I believe God's Word tells us to be salt and light in any generation. We are to flavor our day. We are to shine the light of Jesus into every situation.

> See then that you walk circumspectly, not as fools but as wise, redeeming the time, because the days are evil.
>
> EPHESIANS 5:15–16

If believers aren't faithful to their commitments, their families, and their Lord, then how can we offer hope in any of the negative situations we face today? We are the children of a living God, and we have been challenged to impact our world for Christ. It may take time and practice, but what He has promised, He will perform to the end. That's encouraging!

Chapter 29

Running the Buoys

 For seasoned sailors, a few tips about buoys may seem unnecessary, but a lot of folks on the water have no idea why some of those buoys are painted red and others are painted green.

Most of our lakes and virtually all of our navigable waters contain these channel markers. They mark the path for our boats so that we can stay in the channel. If you head down the wrong side of the buoy, you've got a good chance of running aground or plowing into stumps or rocks. The rule is simple and easy to remember: red on right returning. This means that when you are returning to land, always keep the red markers on your right (and the green ones on your left). To a fisherman running on lakes and rivers, returning home always means going upstream because rivers flow into the sea. Upstream means the red will be on your right.

Because these buoys mark the channel, they can offer clues as to where a good point or drop-off might be located. I especially pay attention to buoys that are situated a long distance from shore. They usually indicate a long point or flat that might hold a lot of fish. The buoys are there for navigational safety, but sometimes they lead to a "honeyhole."

In life, we also have to watch out for the buoys. The devil loves to make us run "outside the channel." He wants us to travel in dangerous, shallow waters. One of Satan's primary goals is to isolate us from other Christians,

and the best way to do that is to keep us out of church. It's really pretty easy to do. Mix up a bit of conflict and add in a few difficult emotions, and some folks will check out and never come back to church.

Without church, your close personal relationship with God will always suffer. Most likely, your relationship will deteriorate until it's no longer close or personal, or it can even end the relationship. Any victory for the devil brings pain and suffering to us.

Just as the red buoys mark the way to return home, the church is the way to return to God. The parable of the lost son (Luke 15) lets us

know that God is always watching for our return. It also assures us that God is waiting with open arms to celebrate our homecoming.

When problems seem to pile up, the answers to your problems might just be down the road at your local church. You may not find a church full of perfect people, but you will find a church full of God. The God I serve is in the business of taking care of those who belong to Him.

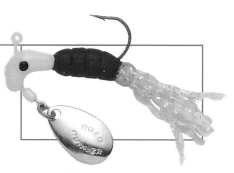

Catch of the *Day*

A lady once approached a minister and explained her reason for not attending church: "Why should I attend your church, pastor? It's overcrowded with hypocrites." The pastor quickly replied, "That's okay, there's always room for one more."

The church is a group of folks who have one common belief in Jesus Christ, and they come together to minister to one another and share the teachings of Christ. There is nothing like the camaraderie, fellowship, love, and support that church members can share with one another in the body of Christ.

> *Now indeed there are many members, yet one body.*
>
> I CORINTHIANS 12:20

Jesus knew that the church was important for believers. He knew it would be necessary for Christians to be empowered, so He offered it through the church. He knew Christians would face opposition, so He promised security in the church. Most of all, He promised He would remove His church from this world before the tribulation began. After all, it is His church.

Chapter 30

Drop Shot

One of the new and exciting fish catching techniques to come along in the last couple of years is the drop shot. It was developed in Japan, migrated quickly to the West coast in tournaments, and now is a staple all across the country.

This technique is similar to the old catfish rigs, which use a bell sinker in the bottom and a hook attached to the line a couple of feet above the weight. We normally just tie a loop in the line and put the hook through the loop. This creates a weak spot in your line, however, where your line can easily break.

On a drop shot, you want to tie the hook on first and leave a long tag line to tie your weight. The tag length can range from ten to twelve inches to six feet or more. I use a Jimmy Houston knot on the hook. After I tie the knot, I run the tag end back through the eye of the hook. From the bend side, this will cause the hook to stand straight out from the line. Next, attach the lead weight and put on a small worm or lizard. Now you're ready to drop shot.

The trick is to keep the lead on the bottom and create a lot of action on the worm by shaking your rod. Normally, the bass won't hit the bait while you're shaking it. The strike comes when you stop and let the bait fall back to the bottom. It's a deadly technique anywhere you would normally use a Carolina rig, even around boat docks.

Drop shotting is one of those techniques that works best in clear water and gives you a few fish when the bite is really tough. A regular catfish or bell sinker will work well on the line, but my friends Rich Tauber and Greg Hinds use a special weight called a Bakudan. This round lead has a built-in clip for your line. You don't need to waste time tying another knot, and if you hang up the weight, it will slide off so you won't lose your hook. Slip on another Bakudan, and you're back to fishin'.

The Bakudan weight is a shortcut to drop shot fishing, but too many times we try to take shortcuts in life. In my experience, shortcuts produce short rewards. There is no substitute for hard work.

The Bible—especially Psalms and Proverbs—is full of great lessons about hard work. Paul, who is perhaps the greatest evangelist of all time, worked for everything he had and provided for all of his helpers.

When I look at successful fishermen, they all have the common trait of being very hard workers. The last trucks at the boat ramp on practice days will be those of the very best fishermen—men like Roland Martin and David Fritts. Though shortcuts can be tempting, the hardest worker will almost always receive the biggest payoff.

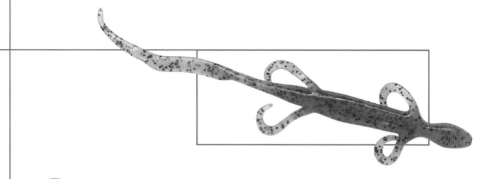

Catch of the **Day**

When the disciples tried to send the crowds away who had gathered to hear the Lord, Jesus told the disciples to feed the people. The disciples were shocked to think about feeding such a large crowd of thousands, but Jesus told them to look for food in the crowd. When they found a boy with only five loaves of

What are

they among

so many?

JOHN 6:9

bread and two fish, Jesus blessed and multiplied that "box lunch" into a fish fry. God works miracles with insignificant amounts every day.

We worry about large plans and schemes. We fret about the proper formula and form. But our Lord wants us to know that He can bless our work for Him in simple, basic ways. When our lives, our efforts, our "fish and loaves," are placed in His hands, multiplied blessings abound. Don't overlook God's ability by hindering it with your inability.